Pocket Guide to

Line Dancing

Terminology

[A Guide for Beginners]

Pocket Guide to Line Dancing Terminology

[A Guide for Beginners]

First Printing November 2018

Second Printing February 2019

ISBN: 9781729419311

Printed and bound in the United States

Cover design provided by Amazon.

Welcome to the world of line dancing!

Line dances are a series of choreographed steps that are repeated until a song or piece of music has finished playing. In a 4-wall line dance you will face a different wall of the room each time you begin the series of steps. For a 2-wall line dance you will begin each series either facing the front (12 o'clock) wall or the back (6 o'clock) wall.

If you have never done any type of organized dancing before, you need to be patient with yourself. Just like learning to read, you need to get a grip on the basics, then practice, practice, practice. Learn one dance, and learn it well, before you try to learn another.

Line dance steps should feel natural. If you take too large a step you will be off balance and it will take longer to complete the step. This results in a situation called "chasing the music" – constantly trying to catch up to the beat.

Please do only what is comfortable for you. Most steps can be adjusted to accommodate physical limitations and personal comfort levels. Your instructor can help you modify any steps that are challenging for you.

Most line dance steps are counted in groups of eight beats. The beats are counted individually as 1, 2, 3, 4, 5, 6, 7, 8, or in double time as 1&2, 3&4, etc. An exception is the waltz, counted 1-2-3, 4-5-6.

New dancers often ask what they should do with their hands or arms while dancing. You can do whatever feels comfortable, keeping in mind that arms should not wave about wildly, endangering nearby dancers. Although there is no standard hand position, here are a few suggestions:

- Hook your thumbs into the front belt loops of your jeans
- Slide your fingertips into your front or back pockets
- Join your hands behind your back (a common position for waltzes)
- At the very least, bend your elbows while you are dancing so your arms don't hang down as if they don't belong to your body. This may feel awkward at first, but it gives you much better form.

And, speaking of form, try not to look at your feet when you dance. You don't need to watch your feet when you walk, so try to send messages to your feet while you keep your head up!

It's okay to follow a more experienced dancer (one who actually knows the dance) when you first start learning, but you want to train your **own** muscles to do the dance. If you constantly watch another dancer, you're training yourself to follow instead of training your body to do the steps.

It's also a good idea to practice your dancing in front of a full-length mirror. That's why dance studios have mirrored walls. If you practice in front of a mirror in your own home, you may feel foolish at first, but your form and technique will improve greatly.

I've noticed three phenomena peculiar to beginning line dancing:

The first phenomenon is that the doorway to your dance venue acts as an invisible barrier; most of what you've learned in the last hour or so stays in the room when you leave. The best way to combat this phenomenon is to practice on your own as much as possible. Try to remember the names of the steps you've been doing. Use this book or the internet to help jog your memory.

Phenomenon number two is the pitfall of getting caught up in the music and trying to sing along as you dance. When you are first learning a dance, your brain can operate your feet or your mouth, but not both. If you try to sing along, your feet become rudderless and don't know what to do on their own. Wait until you know the dance well before you try to add vocals.

The final phenomenon is particularly frustrating: you finally catch on to the dance just as the music ends. If you are in a beginner class or workshop, the instructor may start the dance over again to make sure everyone has grasped it. If not, try to keep doing the dance even after the music ends to make sure you do know it.

Practice is key to everything you want to master!

Not all dance steps are included here, and some steps are known by more than one name (e.g. step-turn/step-pivot). Also, this book does not define steps or positions specific to couples dancing, but the basic steps included here should help all dancers to recognize the language of line dancing.

Amnesia Wall **aka Wallnesia**	The phenomenon of forgetting the dance steps when you start the dance over facing a different wall
Anchor Step **1 1/2 beats** **1&** **(3 steps to 2 beats of music)**	*Right anchor step:* 1) Step ball of right foot behind heel of left foot and put weight on it 2) Return weight to left foot *Left anchor step:* 1) Step ball of left foot behind heel of right foot and put weight on it 2) Return weight to right foot
And **1/2 beat**	A quick step bringing one foot next to the other. The timing for this step is between the beats, as in 1&2.

'And' does not always indicate an actual step. Your instructor or the choreographer may simply be giving you additional information such as 'shuffle and rock,' indicating that you should finish the shuffle, then add a rock step.

Applejacks

4 beats

1) With weight evenly distributed, lift right toes and left heel, swivel toes and heel to right side, forming a 'v' with your feet

2) Return to starting position, weight evenly distributed

3) Lift left toes and right heel, swivel toes and heel to left, forming a 'v' with your feet

4) Return to starting position, weight evenly distributed

Back Weave **4 beats**	This is similar to a **Weave** but begins by crossing one foot *behind* the other. Think: Behind, side, cross, side *To Back Weave right:* 1) Cross left foot slightly *behind* right foot and put your weight on it 2) Step right foot to the right side 3) Cross left foot *over* right 4) Step right foot to the right side *To Back Weave left:* 1) Cross right foot slightly *behind* left foot and put your weight on it 2) Step left foot to the left side 3) Cross right foot *over* left foot 4) Step left foot to the left side
Brush **1 beat**	Move foot forward and upward so the ball of the moving foot makes very light contact with the floor.

Bump **1 beat**	Push the hip forward or back. If you are not a natural 'bumper,' try bending the knee opposite the bumped hip, putting your weight on the leg of the bumping hip. For example, if you want to bump your right hip forward, shift weight to your right leg, keeping the right knee straight, while bending your left knee.
Butterfly **aka Heel Split** **2 beats**	With weight on balls of both feet, 1) Swivel heels away from each other 2) Swivel heels back together
Charleston **4 beats**	1) Kick right foot slightly forward 2) Step slightly back onto right foot 3) Touch left toe back 4) Step forward onto left foot

Charleston

continued

Variation:

1) Step forward on right foot

2) Kick left foot slightly forward

3) Step back onto left foot

4) Touch right toe back

NOTE: This step can also begin by leading with left foot (kick left foot forward...) or by stepping forward on the left foot before kicking. There are many variations for this step.

Chase

2 beats

1&2

(3 steps to 2 beats of music)

This is a **Pivot Turn** followed immediately by a step forward.

If your right foot leads

1) Step forward with your right foot

&) With both feet maintaining contact with the floor, rise up onto the balls of your feet and use the ball of your right foot to push yourself 1/2 turn to your left, switching weight to your left foot

2) Immediately step forward onto your right foot

If your left foot leads

1) Step forward with your left foot

&) With both feet maintaining contact with the floor, rise up onto the balls of your feet and use the ball of your left foot to push yourself 1/2 turn to your right, switching weight to your right foot

2) Immediately step forward onto your left foot

Chassé	Pronounced shah-SAY
aka Side Shuffle	Think: Side, together, side
2 beats	*Right Chassé*
1&2	1) Step right foot to right side
(3 steps to 2 beats of music)	&) Quickly step left foot next to right foot
	2) Step right foot to right side

Chassé	*Left Chassé*
Continued	1) Step left foot to left side
	&) Quickly step right foot next to left foot
	2) Step left foot to left side
	Interesting note: the word 'sashay' is actually an English corruption of the French word 'chassé.'
Chug **1 beat**	Lift knee of one leg while hopping slightly forward with the supporting leg. A *Right Chug* is a right knee up with a small hop on the left foot, while a *Left Chug* is a left knee up with a small hop forward on the right foot.
	The terms **Chug** and **Hitch** are used interchangeably, though their original meanings were different.

Coaster	Think: Back, together, forward
2 beats	*Right Coaster*
1&2	1) Step back on right foot
	&) Step left foot next to right
(3 steps to 2 beats of music)	2) Step forward onto right foot
	Left Coaster
	1) Step back on left foot
	&) Step right foot next to left
	2) Step forward onto left foot
	A Coaster can also begin by stepping forward, but this is rare and usually morphs into a Mambo step.
Cross-eyed Sailor	This is a mis-heard cue (or three). The actual cue is, "Cross, Side, Sailor," but it is such an entertaining concept, I decided to include it here.
4 beats	
(1, 2, 3&4)	
	1) Step one foot across the other
	2) Step the other foot to the side
	3&4) Do a sailor step (See **Sailor**)

Cross Shuffle	*Right Cross Shuffle*
2 beats	Angle your body slightly toward the left corner of the room:
1&2	
	1) Right foot steps forward slightly, crossing over left foot
(3 steps to 2 beats of music)	&) Left foot steps to left side, about even with heel of right foot
	2) Right foot again steps forward slightly, crossing over left foot

Left Cross Shuffle

Angle your body slightly toward the right corner of the room:

1) Left foot steps forward slightly, crossing over right foot

&) Right foot steps to right side, about even with heel of left foot

2) Left foot again steps forward slightly, crossing over right foot

Cross Walk	This is a stylized walk forward.
aka Prissy Walk	

Beats vary	Lift one foot until it is about a quarter-way up the shinbone of the supporting leg before slightly crossing it over the other foot, causing the hips to rotate to a diagonal wall, hence 'prissy.'
Dance Floor Pattern and Etiquette	Because the Dance Floor is for ALL dancers, it is important to be familiar with the way couples and line dancers share the space. Line dancers dance in the center of the floor, while couples dance in a counter-clockwise direction around the outside walls, **using up the corner spaces to avoid crowding the line dancers.**

Couples have the right of way, so don't block their progress.

Watch out for potential collisions. A crowded floor means you'll have to take smaller steps. If you do bump into someone, it is customary to apologize no matter who is at fault.

Etiquette continued	Drinks should NEVER be brought onto the dance floor. Even a small amount of liquid spilled onto a wooden or tile floor will create hazardous dancing conditions.
Fan **2 beats**	*Heel Fan:* Keeping the ball of the foot on the floor 1) Rotate heel outward 2) Return heel to its original position *Toe Fan:* Keeping the heel of the foot on the floor 1) Rotate toe outward 2) Return toe to its original position
Flick **1 beat**	Raise the lower part of your leg behind you, bending at the knee

From the Top	Start the dance from the very beginning. This can occur anywhere in the dance sequence and its purpose is to ensure the dance steps match the music being played.
Grapevine **aka Vine** **3 beats**	Think: Side, behind, side *Right Vine* 1) Step right foot to right side 2) Step left foot behind right foot 3) Step right foot to right side *Left Vine* 1) Step left foot to left side 2) Step right foot behind left foot 3) Step left foot to left side **NOTE:** *A fourth step is usually added (brush, hitch, kick, touch, etc.) to make this step use four beats of music.*

Haystack	This is a mis-heard cue. The actual cue is, **K-Step**.
Heel Fan **2 beats**	Keeping the ball of the foot on the floor 1) Rotate heel outward 2) Return heel to its original position
Heel Jack **Aka Vaudeville** **&1&2** **2 beats in double time**	*Left Heel Jack:* &) Quickly step right foot next to the left foot 1) Extend left heel toward the left diagonal &) Bring left foot back next to the right foot 2) Cross right foot over left foot OR touch right toe next to left foot

Right Heel Jack

&) Quickly step left foot next to right foot

1) Extend right heel toward right diagonal

&) Bring right foot back next to the left foot

2) Cross left foot over right foot

OR touch left toe next to right foot

Heel Split

aka Butterfly

2 beats

With weight on balls of both feet,

1) Swivel heels away from each other

2) Swivel heels back together

Heel Strut

2 beats

A Heel Strut is a stylized walk.

1) Step forward onto heel of foot, toes in the air

2) Keeping heel in contact with the floor, drop your toes to the floor, taking weight onto that foot

Heel Switches

2 beats

1&2

(3 steps to 2 beats of music)

1) Touch heel of one foot forward.

&) Quickly return that foot to its original position as you

2) Touch the opposite heel forward

Hinge Turn

2 beats

A turn that looks as though your body was a door on hinges. There are various ways to do this step. Here are a couple of examples:

Half Hinge

If your weight is on your left foot and instructions call for a Half Hinge to the right:

1) Step right foot to right side with toes pointing to the right wall (this turns your body 1/4 turn to the right)

2) Step forward on left foot with your toes pointing to the right again, making another 1/4 turn right.

Quarter Hinge

As above, but make only 1/8 turn with each step OR

1) Step right foot to right side with toes pointing to the right wall (making 1/4 turn to the right)

2) Step left foot to the left side

Hitch	Lift knee of one leg.
1 beat	A *Right Hitch* brings the right knee up, while a *Left Hitch* is a left knee up.
	The terms *Hitch* and *Chug* are used interchangeably, though their original meanings were different.
Hold	Freeze. Don't move, Maintain the position you are in for the
Beats vary	specified number of beats, usually one beat of music, but may be longer, depending on the choreographer's instructions.

Hook **1 beat**	Bend non-supporting leg at the knee and cross it over the supporting leg just below the knee. You don't have to lift your hooking leg high, just enough so it looks 'hooked.'
Hop **1 beat** **(as &1)**	&) Take a very quick and tiny step forward with one foot 1) Quickly bring the other foot next to the first foot
Jazz Box **aka Jazz Square** **4 beats**	Think: Cross, back, side, forward *Right Jazz Box:* 1) Right foot crosses over left and takes your weight 2) Left foot takes a small step backward 3) Right foot steps to the right side 4) Left foot steps forward (or across the right foot, depending on the choreographer's instructions)

Jazz Box

Continued

Left Jazz Box:

1) Left foot crosses over right and takes your weight

2) Right foot takes a small step backward

3) Left foot steps to the left side

4) Right foot steps forward (or across the left foot, depending on the choreographer's instructions)

After completing a Jazz Box, your feet will have traced an imaginary small square on the floor, stepping on all four corners of the square (starting position counts as the first corner).

NOTE: A Jazz Box/Square can also begin with a step forward or backward.

Jazz Turn

4 beats

As above, but making 1/4 turn left or right.

For example, beginning with your right foot:

1) Right foot crosses over the left and takes your weight

2) Left foot takes a small step backward

3) Right foot turns 1/4 turn right by stepping to the right side with the toes angled to the right

4) Left foot steps forward (or to the side, or across)

If you begin with your left foot:

1) Left foot crosses over the right and takes your weight

2) Right foot takes a small step backward

3) Left foot makes a quarter turn left by stepping to the left side with the toes angled to the left

4) Right foot steps forward (or to the side, or across)

Joey

aka Running Lock Steps

Beats vary

A Running Lock Step is a series of Lock Steps done one after another.

Beginning with the Right foot:

1) Right foot steps forward slightly

&) Left foot steps forward and behind the right heel and takes weight (at this point, the outer side of the left foot will be aligned with the outer side of the right foot)

2) Right foot steps forward again

This is followed immediately by a left lock step:

&) Left foot steps forward slightly

3) Right foot steps forward crossing *behind* the left and takes weight (at this point, the outer side of the right foot will be aligned with the outer side of the left)

&) Left foot steps forward again

Joey **Continued**	For this step, you will constantly change which foot you are using. In the above example, your foot pattern will be:
	Step, lock, step, step, lock, step
	Or:
	right, left, right, left, right, left.
	Definitely takes practice.
K-Step **aka K-Pattern** **8 beats**	A K-Step is a series of step-touches that trace the legs of an imaginary letter **K**. For example:
	1) Step right foot diagonally forward toward right corner
	2) Touch left toes next to right instep (do NOT take weight)
	3) Step left foot diagonally back to original position
	4) Touch right toes next to left instep (do NOT take weight)
	5) Step right foot diagonally back toward right corner

6) Touch left toes next to right instep (do NOT take weight)

7) Step left foot diagonally forward to original position

8) Touch right toes next to left instep (do NOT take weight)

Kick-Ball-Change	1) Low **kick** forward with right foot
2 beats	
1&2	2) Step on **ball** of right foot, next to left foot, taking weight off left
	3) **Change** weight back to left foot
(3 steps to 2 beats of music)	Note: In above example, weight starts and ends on the left foot.
	A Kick-ball-change can also start by kicking with the left foot:
	1) Low **kick** forward with left foot
	2) Step on **ball** of left foot, next to right foot, taking weight off right
	3) **Change** weight back to right foot

Lindy	Chassé combined with a rock back.
4 beats	*To Lindy right*
as 1&2,3,4	1) Step right foot to right side
	&) Quickly step left foot next to right foot
(5 steps to	
4 beats of music)	2) Step right foot to right side
	3) Cross left slightly behind right and put weight on it
	4) Return (recover) weight onto right

To Lindy Left

1) Step left foot to left side

&) Quickly step right foot next to left foot

2) Step left foot to left side

3) Cross right slightly behind left and put weight on it

4) Return (recover) weight onto left

Lock Step

2 beats

1&2

(3 steps to 2 beats of music)

Can also be done as 3 beats for a slower tempo.

Similar to a shuffle step, except that one foot 'locks' behind the other. **Don't lock tightly.** This step is more an illusion than an actual tight lock, which could cause you to trip yourself.

Right Lock Step:

1) Right foot steps forward slightly

&) Left foot steps forward to the *outside* of the right heel and takes weight (at this point, the outer side of the left foot will be lined up with the outer side of the right foot)

2) Right foot steps forward again

Left Lock Step:

1) Left foot steps forward slightly

&) Right foot steps forward to the *outside* of the left heel and takes weight (at this point, the outer side of the right foot will be lined up with the outer side of the left foot)

Lock Step	2) Left foot steps forward again
Continued	A Lock Step can also move backward, 'locking' one ankle **over** the other instead of behind.
LOD/Line of Dance	Circle and couples' dances move around the perimeter of the room and it's important that everyone is moving in the same direction. The Line of Dance always moves counter-clockwise,
Mambo **2 beats** **1&2**	This is a rock step with a bit of hip motion thrown in and, like a rock step, it can be done forward, backward, or to either side.
(3 steps to 2 beats of music)	1) Step out (forward or to the side) on one foot, shifting weight to that foot and bending that knee
	&) Straighten the bent knee as you return your weight to the stationary foot

2) Bring the first foot next to the stationary foot and put weight on it

Bending your knee on the first beat, then releasing it as you return your weight to the stationary foot, will create a bit of hip movement and give this step a mambo feel.

Monterey

4 beats

This step is a series of point-&-step movements with a 1/2 turn (or 1/4 turn) thrown in. Think: point, spin, point, step together. Definitely takes practice.

1) **Point** the toe of your right foot to the right side

2) As you pull your right foot back to the left foot, pivot (**spin**) 1/2 turn on ball of your left foot and step down on right foot, next to left foot

3) **Point** toe of your left foot to the left side

4) Pull left foot in and step next to right foot (**together**)

Monterey

Continued

This step can also begin with a left toe point, in which case the pivot will be to the left.

Also, the spin can be a 1/4 turn instead of 1/2.

Nightclub Basic

2½ beats

as 1, 2, &

1) Step right foot to right side, about shoulder width

2) Rock left foot behind right heel

&) Recover weight onto right foot

Pivot Turn

aka

Step Turn

2 beats

This can be a 1/4 turn or 1/2 turn; occasionally a 3/4 turn.

1) Step forward, taking weight on the balls of both feet

2) **Keeping both feet on the floor**, and using the ball of the forward foot as a 'pusher,' pivot 1/2 turn (or 1/4 turn) shifting your weight onto the opposite foot.

You will find that, depending on which foot takes the forward step, there is only one direction you can turn and still keep both feet on the floor. For example, if you step forward on the right foot, you can only pivot to the left, and the left foot will take your weight.

Try not to over-think this step; you do it naturally every day. If you are leaving the house and suddenly remember you left the coffee pot turned on, you lift onto the balls of your feet and do an about-face, shifting your weight onto your forward foot. That's a *Pivot Turn*!

Point

1 beat

Touch the toe of one foot to the side, but **don't put weight on it**.

To *point right*, extend the right leg out to the side and touch the right toe to the floor.

Likewise, to *point left*, extend the left leg out to the left side and touch the left toe to the floor.

Prissy Walk **aka Cross Walk** **Beats vary**	This is a stylized walk forward. Lift one foot until it is about a quarter-way up the shinbone of the supporting leg before slightly crossing it over the other foot, causing the hips to rotate to a diagonal wall, hence 'prissy.'
Restart **aka** **"From the Top"**	Start the dance from the very beginning. This can occur anywhere in the dance sequence and its purpose is to ensure the dance steps match the music being played.
Rock **2 beats**	This is a weight shift and can be done forward, back, to the right or left side (side rock), or one foot across the other (cross rock), followed by a return to starting position (recover). A rock step always implies a recovery.

	1) Shift weight to the foot that steps forward (or back or to the side)
	2) Return (recover) weight onto the stationary foot
Rocking Chair **aka Rocking Horse** **4 beats**	Two consecutive rock steps – one forward, one back
	1) Step forward on right foot, shifting weight onto right
	2) Return weight to left foot
	3) Step back on right foot, shifting weight onto right foot
	4) Recover weight onto left foot
	Notice in the above example that the left foot never changes position during this step, though you will naturally lift the left heel as you make your forward rock.
	A Rocking Chair can also start on the left foot with the right foot remaining stationary.

Rocking Horse

aka Rocking Chair

Same as Rocking Chair. See above.

Rolling Vine

3 beats

To roll right

1) Step right foot to right side with toes pointing to the right (this turns you 1/4 turn to the right)

2) Step left foot forward with the toes of the left foot pointing to the back wall (when you pick up your right foot you should now be facing the back wall)

3) Continuing to turn to the right, step back on the right foot, making a final 1/2 turn to bring your body back to the starting wall

To roll left

1) Step left foot to left side with toes pointing to the left (this turns you 1/4 turn to the left)

2) Step right foot forward with the toes of the right foot pointing to the back wall (when you pick up

your left foot you should now be facing the back wall)

3) Continuing to turn to the left, step back on the left foot, making a final 1/2 turn to bring your body back to the starting wall

Rumba

2 beats

as 1&2

Rumba Box is the more common step, but some dances call for an abbreviated Rumba Box, which is generally side, together, side:

1) First foot steps to the side

&) Second foot steps next to the first foot

2) First foot steps to side again

Rumba Box

8 beats

(or 4 beats

as 1&2, 3&4)

1) Right foot steps to right side

2) Left foot steps next to right

3) Right foot steps forward

4) Bring left foot next to right but **don't put weight on it**

5) Left foot steps to left side

Rumba Box	6) Right foot steps next to right
Continued	7) Left foot steps back

8) Bring right foot next to left but **don't put weight on it**

There are many variations for a Rumba Box; it can begin on the left foot (left, together, forward), or move backward by stepping back instead of forward on step 3).

Running Lock Step	A Running Lock Step is a series of Lock Steps done one after another.
aka Joey	
Beats vary	

Beginning with the Right foot:

1) Right foot steps forward slightly

&) Left foot steps forward and behind the right heel and takes weight (at this point, the outer side of the left foot will be aligned with the outer side of the right foot)

2) Right foot steps forward again

This is followed immediately by a left lock step:

&) Left foot steps forward slightly

3) Right foot steps forward crossing *behind* the left and takes weight (at this point, the outer side of the right foot will be aligned with the outer side of the left)

&) Left foot steps forward again

For this step, you will constantly change which foot you are using. In the above example, your foot pattern will be:

Step, lock, step, step, lock, step

Or:

right, left, right, left, right, left.

Definitely takes practice.

Sailor Step

2 beats

1&2

(3 steps to 2 beats of music)

Right Sailor Step

1) Sweep right leg out to the side and behind the left leg, taking weight onto the right foot

&) Step left foot slightly to the left side of the right foot

2) Step right foot slightly to the right side of the left foot

Left Sailor Step

1) Sweep left leg out to the side and behind the right leg, taking weight onto the left foot

&) Step right foot slightly to the right side of the left foot

2) Step left foot slightly to the left side of the right foot

If you string several of these steps together, you will resemble a sailor trying to walk on a rocking ship.

Sailor Turn

2 beats

1&2

(3 steps to 2 beats of music)

As above, but with a quarter (sometimes half) turn.

Right Sailor Turn

1) Sweep right leg out to the right side and behind the left leg - use the momentum of this motion to turn your body 1/4 turn to the right, taking weight onto the right foot

&) Step left foot slightly to the left side of right foot

2) Step right foot slightly to the right side of left foot

Left Sailor Step

1) Sweep left leg out to the side left side and behind right leg – use the momentum of this motion to turn your body a 1/4 turn to the left, taking weight onto left foot

&) Step right foot slightly to the right side of left foot

2) Step left foot slightly to the left side of right foot

Scissors	Think: Side, together, cross
2 beats	*Right Scissor Step:*
1&2	1) Right foot steps slightly to the right side
(3 steps to 2 beats of music)	&) Left foot steps next to right while your body angles slightly to the left forward diagonal, which makes it easier to:
	2) Cross right foot over left
	Left Scissor Step:
	1) Left foot steps slightly to the left side
	&) Right foot steps next to left while your body angles slightly to the right forward diagonal, which makes it easier to:
	2) Cross left foot over right
Scuff	Move foot forward and upward, past the foot you are standing on, making light contact on the floor with the heel of the forward-moving foot.
1 beat	
	(Compare to *Brush.*)

Shimmy

A shoulder movement:

2 beats

1&2

Alternately push your right shoulder forward (1), return it to a neutral position as you push your left shoulder (&) forward then return it to a neutral position (2).

For this movement, your arms should be bent at the elbows to give it more styling.

Shuffle

2 beats

Right Shuffle:

1&2

1) Right foot steps forward slightly

(3 steps to 2 beats of music)

&) Left foot steps next to the heel of the right foot and takes weight

2) Right foot steps forward again

Left Shuffle:

1) Left foot steps forward slightly

&) Right foot steps next to the heel of the left foot and takes weight

Shuffle	A Shuffle can also move backward using the same pattern described above; simply step back instead of forward.
Continued	

Side Shuffle	*Right Side Shuffle*
aka Chassé	1) Step right foot to right side
2 beats	&) Quickly step left foot next to right foot
1&2	
	2) Step right foot to right side
(3 steps to 2 beats of music)	*Left Side Shuffle*
	1) Step left foot to left side
	&) Quickly step right foot next to left foot
	2) Step left foot to left side

Skate	This is a diagonal step designed to resemble ice skating.
1 beat	
	To skate with the right foot, trace a *small* arc forward and toward the right corner with your right foot,

then step down on right foot, then put your weight on it. To skate left, trace a _small_ arc forward and toward the left diagonal, then put your weight on it.

Slide **2 beats**	1) Side step slightly wider than shoulder width 2) Draw opposite foot along the floor until it is touching next to the weight-bearing foot but **don't put weight on it** (Unless the choreographer's instructions say otherwise).
Stamp **1 beat**	Bring the foot forcefully down flat onto the floor and immediately lift it up again. In general, people use the terms 'Stomp' and 'Stamp' interchangeably.
Step **1 beat**	Place foot on the floor and take weight onto it

Step Sheet   A **Step Sheet** is a page of
                      notations explaining how to do a
                      particular dance. There is not
                      much standardization on these
                      sheets and they can be very
                      confusing.

                      A Step Sheet gives you a lot of
                      information about the dance: Title,
                      choreographer, the number of
                      steps, what music to use, etc.

                      The dance instructions are usually
                      broken up into sections. The
                      section heading is in bold type (or
                      all capitals or in a larger font) and
                      gives you a summary for 8 counts
                      of the dance. Below this summary
                      is a more detailed description of
                      each of those steps. The next
                      section will show another 8 counts,
                      followed by a more detailed
                      breakdown, and so on, until all the
                      dance steps are represented.

Copperknob.com, Kickit.com and Linedancer.com are great sources for step sheets, and sometimes includes video demonstrations and/or instructional videos.

You can also find step sheets on the sites maintained by the choreographers themselves.

Step Turn

aka Pivot Turn

2 beats

This can be a 1/4 turn or 1/2 turn; occasionally a 3/4 turn.

1) Step forward, taking weight on the balls of both feet

2) **Keeping both feet on the floor**, and using the ball of the forward foot as a 'pusher,' pivot 1/2 turn (or 1/4 turn) shifting your weight onto the opposite foot.

You will find that, depending on which foot takes the forward step, there is only one direction you can turn and still keep both feet on the floor. For example, if you step forward on the right foot, you can only pivot to the left, and the left foot will take your weight.

Step Turn **Continued**	Try not to over-think this step; you do it naturally every day. If you are leaving the house and suddenly remember you left the coffee pot turned on, you lift onto the balls of your feet and do an about-face, shifting your weight onto your forward foot. That's a *Step Turn*!
Stomp **1 beat**	Bring the foot down forcefully, flat onto the floor, and put your weight on it. To make the stomp more satisfying, let the heel of your boot do the work, making a sharp sound on the wood floor.
	WARNING: If you are not wearing boots, be gentle with yourself. Trying to make a sharp sound on a hard floor while wearing rubber- or soft-soled shoes can cause you a lot of pain, either right away or the following day. And be aware: whether or not you are wearing boots, many tile or linoleum floors are laid over concrete, making stomping hazardous to your bones and joints.

Stroll

8 beats

A **Stroll** combines elements of a grapevine, a hinge turn, and a back weave.

Strolling to the right:

1) Right foot steps to right side

2) Left foot crosses behind right

3) Right foot steps to right side with toes pointing to the right (this makes a 1/4 turn to the right, the 3 o'clock wall)

4) Left foot steps forward toward the 3 o'clock wall, with the toes pointing toward the 6 o'clock wall (this makes another quarter turn to the right - you will now be facing the 6 o'clock wall)

5) Right foot crosses behind left foot

6) Left foot steps to left side

7) Right foot crosses over left foot

8) Left foot steps to left side

Stroll **Continued**	Strolling to the left simply reverses the steps above, beginning with the left foot stepping to the left side.
	To make a long story short, think: Side, behind, quarter, quarter, behind, side, cross, side
	The Stroll was a popular party dance in the 50's and 60's. For those who remember the dance, this is the same patterned step.
Strut	See 'Heel Strut' or 'Toe Strut.'
Sugar Foot **2 beats** **1&2** **(3 steps to 2 beats of music)**	*Right Sugar Foot:* 1) Touch toes of right foot next to instep of left foot &) Touch heel of right foot next to instep of left foot 2) Step forward onto right foot

Left Sugar Foot:

1) Touch toes of left foot next to instep of right foot

&) Touch heel of left foot next to instep of right foot

2) Step forward onto left foot

Sugar Push

2 beats

1&2

As above, but 2) steps across instead of forward.

Sweep

Foot traces a semi-circular pattern on the floor as it crosses in front of (or behind) the other foot.

Swivel

Beats vary

With weight on balls of feet, heels swing to the right (or left) and take your weight. Toes then swing to the right and weight shifts back to the balls of your feet. Alternate heel and toe movements to move yourself across the floor.

Swivet	1) With weight evenly distributed, lift right toes and left heel, swing right toes to the right and left heel to the left side (toes of both feet should be angled to the right; heels should be angled to the left).
2 beats	
as 1&2&	
(4 steps to 2 beats of music)	&) Return to starting position, weight evenly distributed
	2) Lifting left toes and right heel, swing left toes to the left and right heel to the right side (toes of both feet should be angled to the left; heels should be angled to the right).
	&) Return to starting position
Tag	Some dances employ a **Tag** to use up extra beats of music. These are additional steps inserted into the dance and vary according to the choreographer's directions. Check the **step sheet** for instructions.
Beats vary	
Tap	Touch toe (or heel) to the floor but <u>don't put any weight on it</u>.
aka Touch	
1 beat	

Tap & Go	Think: tap, step
2 beats	1) Touch the ball of your foot to the floor in front of you
	2) Lift that foot and step down, putting your weight on it
	[Compare to Toe Strut]
Toe Fan	*Toe Fan:*
2 beats	Keeping the heel of the foot on the floor
	1) Rotate the toe outward
	2) Return toe to its original position
Toe Strut	1) Dig your toe into the floor and, **without lifting the toe off the floor**
2 beats	
	2) Drop your heel onto the floor
	[Compare to Tap & Go]

Toe Switches 2 beats	1) Touch toes of one foot out to the side. &) Quickly return that foot to its original position as you 2) Touch the opposite toes to the other side
Together aka Close 1 beat	The foot that steps 'together' steps next to the weight-bearing foot and **takes your weight**.
Touch aka Tap 1 beat	Touch toe or heel to the floor but <u>don't put any weight on it</u>.
Triple Half 2 beats 1&2 (3 steps to 2 beats of music)	Three quick steps (right, left, right OR left, right, left) as you make a half turn in place.

Triple Step **2 beats** **1&2** **(3 steps to 2 beats of music)**	Three quick steps in place: right, left, right OR left, right, left. In general, a triple step stays in one place, though it can move forward or backward according to the choreographer's directions.
Twinkle **3 beats**	A Waltz pattern in which the first foot crosses over the weight-bearing foot. For example, if your weight is on your right foot: 1) Cross left over right and put your weight on it 2) Step right foot to right side 3) Step left foot next to right foot Think: Cross, side, together
V-Block **aka V-Pattern** **aka V-Step** **4 beats**	Can begin on either the left or the right foot, and traces a 'V' pattern on the floor: out, out, in, in.

V-Block	For example, if right foot leads:
Continued	1) Right foot steps forward to a slight right diagonal
	2) Left foot steps forward to a slight left diagonal
	3) Right foot steps back to its original position
	4) Left foot steps next to right
Vaudeville	*Left Vaudeville:*
aka Heel Jack	&) Quickly step right foot next to the left foot
2 beats	
&1&2	1) Extend left heel toward the left diagonal
	&) Bring left foot back next to the right foot
2 beats in double time	
	2) Cross right foot over left foot
(4 steps to 2 beats of music)	OR touch right toe next to left foot

Right Vaudeville:

&) Quickly step left foot next to right foot

1) Extend right heel toward right diagonal

&) Bring right foot back next to the left foot

2) Cross left foot over right foot

OR touch left toe next to right foot

Vine Jack

4 beats

1, 2, &3&4

This is a Grapevine that becomes a *Heel Jack* (*Vaudeville*).

Left Vine Jack:

1) Left foot steps to the left side

2) Right foot crosses behind left

&) Quickly step left foot next to right foot

3) Extend right heel toward right diagonal

&) Quickly return right foot next to left foot

Vine Jack **Continued**	4) Cross left foot over right OR touch left toe next to right

Right Vine Jack

1) Right foot steps to right side

2) Left foot crosses behind right

&) Quickly step right foot next to left foot

1) Extend left heel toward left diagonal

&) Quickly return left foot next to right foot

2) Cross right foot over left

OR touch right toe next to left foot

Walk **Beats vary**	Exactly what it sounds like. Step forward (or back, according to the dance instructions). ***Walk*** is included here because new dancers sometimes think it might mean something different from an everyday sort of walk. It doesn't.

Wall

This is the wall you face at any given point in the dance.

Imagine you are standing at the center of a clock face. The wall directly in front of you (your starting wall) is the 12 o'clock wall. Directly behind you is the 6 o'clock wall. To your right is 3 o'clock, and 9 o'clock is to your left. Instructors and choreographers use these walls to clarify which wall a dancer should face at a particular point in the dance. This is especially helpful when turns or tricky choreography leaves you wondering which wall you should face (called 'losing your wall').

Waltz step

3 beats

Think: long, short, short

For a Basic Waltz step:

1) Step left foot forward

2) Step right foot next to left

3) Step left foot in place.

Waltz step **Continued**	Another way to think of this pattern is 'forward, together, together.' When waltzing, your feet will constantly alternate as LEFT, right, left; RIGHT, left, right, etc.
	Any 3-beat step can be done to a waltz beat (grapevine, coaster, chase, etc.)
Weave **4 beats**	Begins with a cross step. Think: Cross, side, behind, side.
	To *Weave Right*
Compare to **Back Weave**	1) Cross left foot in front of right foot and put your weight on it
	2) Right foot steps to right side
	3) Left foot crosses behind right
	4) Right foot steps to right side
	To *Weave Left*
	1) Cross right foot in front of left foot and put your weight on it

2) Left foot steps to left side

3) Right foot crosses behind left

4) Left foot steps to left side

Wizard

2 1/2 beats

1, 2&

(3 steps to 2 beats of music)

A Wizard step is much like a Lock Step, but the tempo is different. Think of The Wizard of Oz movie and the way Judy Garland danced down the Yellow Brick Road.

Right Wizard Step:

1) Right foot steps forward slightly

2) Left foot steps forward to the *outside* of the right heel and takes weight (at this point, the outer side of the left foot will be lined up with the outer side of the right foot)

&) Right foot quickly steps forward

Left Wizard Step:

1) Left foot steps forward slightly

2) Right foot steps forward to the *outside* of the left heel and takes weight (at this point, the outer side of the right foot will be lined up with the outer side of the left foot)

&) Left foot quickly steps forward

Remember, practice is the key.

Now one more time...

...From The Top.

.

Printed in Great Britain
by Amazon